I0605132

POLITICAL SYSTEMS IN ACTION

SOCIALISM

From the Industrial Revolution to the Trade Union

ALEX WEBB

CHERITON CHILDREN'S BOOKS

Published in 2025 by **Cheriton Children's Books**
1 Bank Drive West, Shrewsbury, Shropshire, SY3 9DJ, UK

First Edition

Author: Alex Webb
Designer: Paul Myerscough
Editor: Sarah Eason
Proofreader: Anna Chambers

Picture credits: Cover: Doodle Press. Inside: p4: Shutterstock/Just Another Photographer, p5: Shutterstock/Hadrian, p6: Shutterstock/Vangelis Aragiannis, p9: Wikimedia Commons/Jan Gumpinger, p10: Shutterstock/Everett Collection, p11: Shutterstock/Everett Collection, p12: Wikimedia Commons/University of Liverpool Faculty of Health & Life Sciences, p13: Wikimedia Commons/Leon Perskie, p14: Shutterstock/Mark Reinstein, p15: Alamy/Agencja Fotograficzna Caro, p16: Shutterstock/Attila Jandi, p17: Wikimedia Commons/Hans Holbein the Younger, p18: Shutterstock/LightField Studios, p19: Shutterstock/Kordin Viacheslav, p20: Shutterstock/Maridav, p21: Shutterstock/Rob Crandall, p22: Shutterstock/Dylan Hatfield, p23: Wikimedia Commons/LSE Library, p24: Shutterstock/Tupungato, p25: Shutterstock/Iryna Inshyna, p26: Shutterstock/Everett Collection, p27: Shutterstock/Everett Collection, p28: Wikimedia Commons/Library of Congress, p29: Wikimedia Commons, p30: Shutterstock/Talukdar David, p31: Wikimedia Commons/Yousuf Karsh, p32: Shutterstock/Rieke Photos, p33: Wikimedia Commons/Library of Congress, p34: Shutterstock/Northfoto, p35: Shutterstock/Bene A, p37: Shutterstock/LMspencer, p38: Shutterstock/David Fowler, p39: Wikimedia Commons/Los Angeles Daily News, p41t: Shutterstock/JBula_62, p41b: Shutterstock/Lev Radin, p42: Shutterstock/Thanasis F, p43: Shutterstock/Boonkung, p44: Shutterstock/Ground Picture, p45: Shutterstock/UfaBizPhoto.

Printed in the United States of America

Contents

CHAPTER 1

The Story of Socialism

Television and the media are often full of stories about fabulously rich people and the wonderful lives they lead with their huge houses, amazing clothes, and private jets. You may have seen these stories and thought, "That's not fair, why do these people have more than me?" You might have learned about the millions of people living in poverty in the world's poorest countries and thought it unfair that some people have so much and others so little. What do these thoughts have to do with socialism, and what is socialism?

Making Society More Equal

Socialism is a political and economic system with the key aim of making society more equal. However, the supporters of socialism do not always agree about the best ways to achieve this ideal goal. There are different socialist "schools of thought" about how best to build a fair society. Some people oppose socialism. In fact, many people in western societies support capitalism and do not agree with socialism. Opponents of socialism claim that socialist societies are just as unfair as capitalist societies, such as the United States, but simply unfair in different ways.

The Workers Movement Memorial in Budapest, Hungary. Socialists believe that workers should join together to gain more power in society.

People protesting on the streets of Paris, France, against rising taxes and increasing poverty

Ideas Around the World

Socialist ideas are present in many governments around the world today. Socialists usually believe that society will be fairer if more aspects of it are controlled by the state, or government. Some areas that governments control are education, transportation, and housing. Socialism is an influence when governments provide a welfare system or free medical care. Socialism can help the poorer people in society by improving education, housing, and creating job opportunities. In some countries, socialism—and its more extreme form communism—results in societies that severely restrict the freedom and actions of individual citizens. There, force is used to make people follow socialism.

SOCIALISM: PAST AND PRESENT

In this book we will look at the political system of socialism, its history, and its place in the world today. We'll compare socialism past with socialism present, and look at some of the key figures of this political system in the People and Politics features. Look out too for the Socialism in Action features throughout the book and try to answer the questions that accompany some of them.

Socialism and the Industrial Revolution

Socialist ideas first started to appeal to large numbers of people during the Industrial Revolution. This was a time of enormous change, in which inventions in machinery changed the way people worked forever. The Industrial Revolution swept across Europe and North America from the late 1700s onward. However, the roots of socialism were probably laid long before the Industrial Revolution took hold. The vision of socialism comes from the time when ancient thinkers turned their attention to dreaming up the ideal of an equal society.

Ancient Ideas

The earliest socialist ideas can be traced back to the ancient Greek thinker, Plato (c.427–348 BCE). Plato wrote *The Republic*, in which he imagined an ideal society. In this society people shared their property. Plato put forward the idea of a society in which the ruling class lived communally without private property or families. The ruling class were named the Guardians.

Plato suggested that the Guardians give up personal wealth to prevent arguments and corruption. Although this is not socialism in the modern sense, it does introduce the idea of collective ownership and communal living. This shared ownership was also a feature of early Christian communities, such as monasteries.

A statue of Plato

A Changing World

By the late 1800s, societies in Europe and North America were starting to change. Steam power was being used in large factories that employed hundreds of people. To work in the factories, people moved from rural areas to live in huge and ever-growing cities. The American and French Revolutions of the late 1700s also had a huge impact on political ideas. They spread the idea that "all men are created equal," but the ideal did not usually include women and slaves. It would take many more years for the benefits of equality to extend to those two groups. The ideas that sprang up in the 1700s and 1800s laid the foundations for the development of socialism.

The Spread of Ideas

The early socialists, such as the Diggers, lived in small communities. The Diggers were a group of poor farming people who lived in the 1600s in England. They believed they should have the right to farm the land freely, without payment to wealthy landowners.

By the 1800s, when socialist ideas began to gain popularity in new industrial cities, society was very different. Some of the changes that were taking place included people moving to live in cities and changing the type of work they did. As more people lived in towns and cities, it became easier to share ideas —ideas such as socialism.

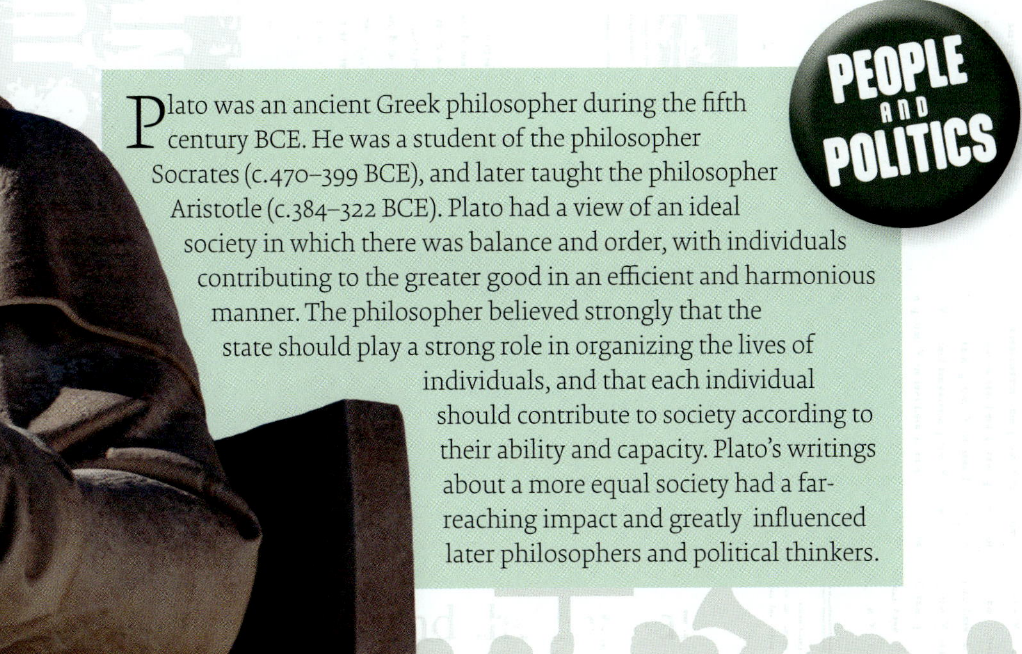

PEOPLE AND POLITICS

Plato was an ancient Greek philosopher during the fifth century BCE. He was a student of the philosopher Socrates (c.470–399 BCE), and later taught the philosopher Aristotle (c.384–322 BCE). Plato had a view of an ideal society in which there was balance and order, with individuals contributing to the greater good in an efficient and harmonious manner. The philosopher believed strongly that the state should play a strong role in organizing the lives of individuals, and that each individual should contribute to society according to their ability and capacity. Plato's writings about a more equal society had a far-reaching impact and greatly influenced later philosophers and political thinkers.

Needing a Lot of Money

Building and running the factories and mills of the Industrial Revolution required a lot of money, or capital. The businesspeople, who had capital to invest, became as rich as kings by selling the new manufactured goods that flowed from their factories. While these capitalists counted their money, the men, women, and often children who worked for them counted the cost. They worked very long hours in dangerous conditions for little money. Children as young as four spent up to ten hours a day working in factories or in mines, just to be able to earn enough money to survive.

Socialism Appears

The word "socialist" began to appear in the 1820s. Its meaning was the opposite of the word "capitalist," which meant great profit made by one or a few individuals. In socialism, the ideal was that factories would be owned in common, or by society, rather than by a few capitalists. The theory was that wealth created by the factories would be distributed among the workers.

PEOPLE AND POLITICS

Two German philosophers named Karl Marx (1818–1883) and Friedrich Engels (1820–1895) were the most important figures in the development of socialism. In 1848, they published *The Communist Manifesto*, which included their ideas about how society should be organized. Marx and Engels were critical of capitalism. They called upon the working class to unite and fight against the capitalist system and those in charge. They believed revolution would lead to a classless society with greater freedom.

This statue of Marx and Engels was erected in a public park in Berlin dedicated to the philosophers.

Meaning the Same Thing

To Marx and Engels, communism and socialism were the same thing. They believed that history was all about the struggle between the ruling class, who owned farms and factories, and the working class, who owned nothing. Marx believed that when workers realized this, they would rise up against the oppressive ruling class.

Socialism in Action

These are the last words of *The Communist Manifesto*:

> "The proletariat [working class] have nothing to lose but their chains. They have a world to win. Working men of the world, unite."

The working people were not literally in chains, so what do you think the authors, Friedrich Engels and Karl Marx, meant by these words?

How do they suggest the working class can be successful?

PAST AND PRESENT:

Do you think the words of Engels and Marx have a meaning in the world of today? Give reasons for your answer.

Rise of the Revolutionists

In the later years of the 1800s, socialist political parties began to form in countries across Europe. These early socialists believed, like Karl Marx, that they would only be able to have a say in society by defeating the ruling classes. One of the most extreme of these revolutionary socialists was Vladimir Lenin, the leader of Russia's Bolshevik Party.

PEOPLE AND POLITICS

Vladimir Lenin (1870–1924) founded a political group called the Bolsheviks, which later became the Russian communist party. During his teenage years, Lenin's older brother had been killed for plotting to assassinate Tsar Alexander III and Lenin became heavily influenced by the ideas of Karl Marx. Lenin went on to become the leader of the world's first communist state, the Soviet Union.

Vladimir Lenin

The Chance Comes for War

Lenin's chance for revolution came in 1917. World War I (1914–1918) had been raging across Europe for three years when the Russian people overthrew Tsar Nicholas II. A temporary government was put in place. However, food was in short supply, prices were rising, and the Russian people's wish for control of more land was not met. After a year of revolution, Lenin and his group of fighters seized power. They promised the Russians land, and an end to war and food shortages. Lenin was determined to turn Russia into the world's first communist country —the Soviet Union.

This photograph captures a Bolshevik parade in St Petersburg, Russia, during the Russian Revolution of 1917.

Terrified by Revolution

While communism in Russia inspired many socialists, others were put off the ideal as Russia became a communist dictatorship, which terrorized many of its own people. After World War I, many countries had also given working people the vote, so other socialist political parties focused their attention on gathering votes rather than planning revolution. In the post-war era, countries faced tough economic conditions. That enabled some socialist parties, such as the British Labour Party, to grow. However, socialism came under attack from fascist parties in many countries, which used economic hardship to further their own causes.

Socialism in Action

In the 1800s, ordinary working people, who might vote for socialist political parties, could not vote in elections in most countries. The ruling class was unlikely to vote for socialist political parties that threatened to remove much of their power.

How do you think the ruling classes felt about the spread of socialist ideas?

What do you think happened when people, including women, were free to vote in the early twentieth century? How may that have led to a change in politics?

Socialism Spreads

The United States and the United Kingdom (UK) became allies of the Soviet Union as they battled against Germany, Italy, and Japan in World War II (1939–1945). At the end of the war, Germany was divided into two—East and West. A Soviet-style communist regime was set up in East Germany and across much of eastern Europe. Western nations were determined to stand against what they saw as the evil of communism. However, as people recovered from war, socialist ideas and parties were accepted in many countries.

Owned by the State

In Britain, the government of Sir Winston Churchill, which had led Britain through the war, was replaced by the Labour Party and Prime Minister Clement Attlee. This socialist government took many areas of industry and business into public ownership, meaning that they were owned and run by the state. They also launched a National Health Service (NHS), which was paid for through taxes and was free for all citizens of the country. These acts showed socialists that the capitalist system could be changed by elected politicians rather than revolution.

Socialist Push

After World War II, socialist governments were elected in many countries including Sweden, Denmark, and France. In 1949, Mao Zedong's communists took power in China, in the Far East. Other communist regimes followed, including the Cuban government that was led by leader Fidel Castro.

Aneurin Bevan, Minister for Health in Clement Attlee's Labour government, meets a patient on the first day of the NHS.

Socialism in Action

In the years after 1929, the United States and much of the world was hit by the Great Depression. Many businesses failed and one-quarter of Americans could not find work. There were no welfare payments at the time, and millions of people could not afford to buy enough food to survive. President Franklin D. Roosevelt introduced the "New Deal" to provide more jobs for people. Roosevelt's New Deal was the largest, most expensive government plan in the history of the United States.

Many people saw Roosevelt's New Deal as a socialist act. Why do you think this was?

PAST AND PRESENT: Can you think of similar acts that have taken place in modern times in nonsocialist countries to try to help people during times of hardship?

PEOPLE AND POLITICS

Franklin D. Roosevelt (1882–1945) was the thirty-second president of the United States and ruled the country for 12 years. Although US presidents are now limited to two terms, Roosevelt was elected four times. He led the United States through the Great Depression of the 1930s and through World War II. The policies of his "New Deal" helped stabilize the economy and improve the lives of the poorest American people.

Franklin D. Roosevelt

Politics in Crisis

By the 1970s, it seemed to many people that socialism was replacing capitalism in some countries. However, social democracy —which had been a feature of many democratic countries— and the hardline communism of the Soviet Union were in crisis.

Socialism Stops Success?

In the late 1970s, critics of socialist ideas in western countries, such as the United States and Europe, grew louder. They argued that socialist measures, such as publicly owned businesses and free healthcare, were costly and inefficient. Two of the most prominent supporters of this argument were US president Ronald Reagan, who held office from 1981 until 1989, and British prime minister Margaret Thatcher. The two politicians attracted votes from people who felt that welfare spending, and the high taxes needed to pay for it, had stopped individuals from achieving personal success.

Turning Away from Socialism

In 1989, the communist governments across Eastern Europe crumbled because of economic problems and people's wish to have the freedom they saw in the West. At the end of World War II, the German capital Berlin had been divided into two, like the country. In 1990, the 28-mile-long (45-km-long) Berlin Wall that split Berlin was breached. East and West Germany then merged to form a unified country. The Soviet Union broke up in 1991. Today, there are still communist or socialist governments in some countries, notably China, but many formerly socialist countries have adopted a capitalist system.

PEOPLE AND POLITICS

Ronald Reagan (1911–2004) was the fortieth president of the United States. Favoring capitalism over socialism, his policies reduced the role of the government in economic affairs and the government's responsibility for social problems. Reagan lowered taxes and reduced government restrictions on both business and individuals. Internationally, Reagan was fiercely opposed to the spread of communism.

Ronald Reagan

East and West Berliners gathered on the Berlin Wall in November 1989 to demand freedom of movement.

Socialism in Action

These words were spoken by Ronald Reagan and summed up his view that capitalism would always be more successful than socialism:

> "Socialists ... can provide you shelter, fill your belly with bacon and beans, treat you when you're ill, all the things guaranteed to a prisoner or a slave. They don't understand that we also dream."

What did Reagan mean by saying that we also dream?

What do we dream about that socialism can't provide?

PAST AND PRESENT:

Do you think Reagan was right to say that socialism cannot provide dreams? Do you think that capitalism serves people's dreams today? Give reasons for your answer.

CHAPTER 2

Different Types of Socialism

The history of socialism shows that the political idea has many different strands and variations. Even in the early days of socialism, different thinkers developed their own socialist theories. As socialism has spread around the world and adapted to different cultures, it has also changed. Socialists today share many beliefs, but they disagree on many things, including how much they can compromise with capitalist society.

Around the World

We can see different types of socialism in different parts of the modern world. At one extreme is North Korea. This secretive state still clings to an extreme form of communism. This has brought its people severe poverty and little food, while the country's resources are spent on its armed forces and the cult of its leaders. Food in the country is grown on collective farms. The government takes a large percentage of the food, leaving the rest for farmers.

In North Korea, an extreme form of communism governs the country, promoting strength, unity, and fierce self-reliance, as shown in these political posters.

Socialist Ideals

At the other extreme, there is some evidence of socialist ideals in almost any country that provides its people with free education, welfare payments if they are out of work, or any state-funded healthcare insurance. Many people who would never call themselves socialist still believe that the state should provide state-funded programs to support citizens who need them. Between these two socialist extremes are countries that are governed by democratic socialist regimes, such as Brazil.

Socialism in Action

In 1516, English statesman and humanist, Thomas More (1478–1535), wrote a book called *Utopia*, to show ways in which society could be improved. *Utopia* describes an island on which land and houses were the common property of all the people. On the island, people swap houses every ten years so they do not envy each other's property. Money does not exist and people can take any food and other goods they need from a general store on the island.

Do you think the society described in *Utopia* could ever work? If not, what might stop it from working?

PAST AND PRESENT:

We are seeing huge technological changes in society today, including the advancement of Artificial Intelligence (AI). Some people argue that AI may be able to take over most jobs, so that people would not need to work. Do you think that socialism could become more popular if this is the case?

Thomas More

What Is Democratic Socialism?

The focus of this book is democratic socialism, also known as social democracy. This is the form of socialism followed by mainstream socialist parties in democratic countries around the world. Social democracy grew from the same roots as more extreme revolutionary forms of socialism. However, social democrats disagree strongly with the idea that socialism can be forced on a country through revolution.

Elections Are Best

Social democrats argue that democratic elections and processes are the best way to introduce socialist ideas. To win an election, socialist politicians must explain how they will make life better for the people they want to vote for them. Through election campaigns, political candidates must win the votes of people in society by promising to provide them with what they want.

Regulating the Economy

In a social democracy, the government regulates the economy but it does not have complete control of it. There are different types of financial assistance for citizens, such as welfare or pensions, and basic services such as healthcare and education. Progressive taxes help to redistribute wealth, so the very wealthy pay more, to help the poorest in society live a better life.

In a democratic process, people decide which politicians or party they would like to lead their country.

In a social democracy, the government tries to reduce social inequality.

Involved in People's Lives

Social democrats believe that the state should be more closely involved in people's lives, either by owning important businesses directly, or by making sure that they follow government rules. Social democrats pass laws to ensure that workers are treated fairly. To help them achieve these goals, the governments must spend more money, so they ask the people to pay taxes. The next chapter explains how this type of socialism works.

Socialism in Action

There are many questions people ask themselves when they're deciding who to vote for in an election. Two of these questions are:

- Which party will make them richer? Socialist parties will normally ask wealthier people to pay more taxes, but they will provide more government services to people who have less money.
- Which government will provide the best schools, hospitals, and other services? Some people believe that these services are better if they are managed by the state. Others feel that private companies will serve customers more effectively to make bigger profits.

Which of the above issues and benefits are important to you and why?

Socialism and Revolution

Revolutionary socialists, or communists, are not concerned about getting elected. Like the first communist government in the Soviet Union, they take power by force rather than waiting to be elected. They follow the Marxist idea that society is engaged in a constant struggle between workers and the ruling or capitalist class.

The Most Extreme Socialism

Communism is an extreme form of socialism in which most, or all, property in a country is owned by its government. People who live in communist countries do not normally have any choice about who governs them. Most communist governments around the world took power many years ago, often with the support of the Soviet Union. Some countries, like China, have allowed private businesses to embrace capitalism. A few Chinese citizens have become wealthy. Socialists would argue that these citizens are, in fact, not socialist at all.

Change in Czechoslovakia

In 1948, in the country of Czechoslovakia, communists supported by the Soviet Union carried out a coup, or military takeover. Leading politicians who supported democracy were arrested and imprisoned, and the communists then infiltrated the Czech government. The Czech president was forced from power and replaced by the leader of the communist party. In the late 1980s protests in the country resulted in the communist government giving up power and, elections were held in 1990. Soon afterward, the country split into two independent countries, Slovakia and the Czech Republic.

In China, economic growth has brought more freedom for the country's citizens, but the government still has tight controls.

Fidel Castro (1926–2016) introduced an extreme form of socialism to Cuba in the late 1950s.

Power in Cuba

Cuba is one of the last communist regimes. Fidel Castro took power in Cuba after a revolution in 1959. Castro introduced communism to Cuba, and took total control of the country. Castro argued that by taking control of the country he improved education and healthcare for most Cubans. During the Cold War, Cuba was closely allied with the Soviet Union, a great threat to the United States at the time. As a result, Cuba still faces sanctions from the United States. In 2006, Fidel Castro handed over power to his brother, Raul, who reformed Cuba so it was easier for businesses to operate there. Then in 2018, Raul stepped down at the age of 86, and his former bodyguard Miguel Díaz-Canel took over on his behalf.

Socialism in Action

Social democracy is the most common form of modern socialism, while communism is sometimes called "revolutionary socialism." Look back at pages 18–21 to see some of the similarities and differences between these forms of socialism.

How does a communist government take power? How does this differ from the government in a social democracy?

How are individuals treated in a communist society or in a social democracy? What are some advantages and disadvantages of each system of government?

Unusual Forms of Socialism

Social democracy and communism have been the most common branches of socialism, but socialist ideas have often been adapted by other groups to suit their own campaigns. These groups include Christians, who favored socialism because they felt that capitalism went against Christian teaching.

Without State Control

Anarcho-socialists are opposed to all forms of state control. They believe that without the control of the state, people will naturally cooperate with each other. This idea has never been tested in a whole country, but has been trialed by small groups. Anarcho-socialism was a feature of some small socialist groups, or communes, in the 1960s. It has also been used to justify terrorist acts against the state, such as those carried out by Red Brigades in Italy during the 1970s. The group carried out more than 50 attacks against the state, including murders and kidnappings. The aim was to weaken and overthrow the Italian government and set up a revolutionary society run by the lower social classes.

Do Not Trust

Syndicalists had a similar distrust of the state. They were an extreme wing of the trade union movement, who were particularly active in the early 1900s. In trade unions, workers come together to argue for better pay and working conditions. Syndicalists believed that, through direct action and general strikes across many industries, they could destroy the government. Afterward, workers could control their own factories.

Mikhail Bakunin (1814–1876) was the founder of anarcho-socialism. He fought against capitalism, government, and religion.

Socialism in Action

In the nineteenth century, many people questioned the right of women to vote. They argued that women didn't have the training for good political judgment and were better suited to running a home and raising children. Campaigners for women's voting rights often supported socialist ideas.

What aspects of socialism do you think helped the campaign for women's rights?

What impact do you think World War I had on the women's rights movement? How did society change during these years?

Emmeline Pankhurst

PEOPLE AND POLITICS

British activist Emmeline Pankhurst (1858–1928) famously campaigned for 40 years to secure equal voting rights for women as leader of the "suffragettes." She was also an advocate for better working conditions for women. Emmeline was imprisoned many times for her involvement in political protests. Just days after her death, aged 69, women were given equal voting rights, at the age of 21.

CHAPTER 3

How Socialism Works

What is it like to live in a country run on socialist principles? Although all socialist political parties have slightly different ideas about how to put socialist ideas into practice, they do share certain beliefs about how to make countries more equal and fairer.

Living in a Socialist Country

Some socialists are prepared to accept compromise with capitalism. This has been particularly true since the collapse of communist regimes and the decline of socialism in the 1980s and 1990s. As the world progresses and globalization takes hold, many countries have embraced some form of capitalism within their societies.

Socialism in Sweden

Sweden is a country of 10.5 million people in northern Europe. The country had a socialist government for much of the twentieth century and is a good example of the principles of socialism in action. A socialist leader in the 1930s described Sweden as "a good home" which "does not consider anyone as privileged or underappreciated."

Social democrats display campaign posters in Stockholm, Sweden, before a general election.

Practicing a Fair Deal

This idea of fairness was put into practice as Sweden devoted a high proportion of the country's wealth to providing health and education systems that would reduce inequality between people. The socialist party was extremely popular for many years, but was helped by strong trade unions that supported the rights of workers. Although the Swedish government did not take over businesses like other socialist countries, it worked with industry to ensure that workers were well treated, and had a say in how the businesses they worked in were run.

In Sweden, high taxation means that compulsory schooling for all children is well funded. Families also have a right to choose or change schools.

Changing with the Times

Like many countries that once embraced socialism, Sweden has changed. However, it still keeps many of its socialist policies in place. The rest of this chapter looks, in more detail, at different socialist policies.

Socialism in Action

In a socialist society, the government provides citizens with a series of universal services and benefits. But they need a sufficient supply of money to do this. In some countries, such as Sweden, Finland, and Denmark, citizens are among the highest tax payers in the world.

Why do you think people in some social democracies are happy to hand over so much of what they earn in taxes to the government?

What do they expect to get in return?

If taxes were lowered, what would be the advantages and disadvantages to the country's citizens?

This photograph was taken in 1909. It shows a young boy working in a cotton mill factory in Vermont.

Exploiting the Workers

The concern that workers were being exploited in factories, and other businesses, was one of the main reasons for the spread of socialist ideas. Public ownership of industries and the issues that surround it has been a central feature of many socialist governments.

During the Industrial Revolution, workers lacked many of the things that employees today expect. There were no laws to stop children working in dangerous jobs, and there were no benefits, such as limited working hours and paid vacation. Most socialists felt that the only way to achieve better conditions was for workers to limit the power of private owners.

Socialism in Action

In the United States, most businesses are owned and managed by private individuals, although there may be strict regulations from government about how they operate. Workers in these types of businesses may have lower pay or fewer vacations than those in nationalized businesses elsewhere. However, private businesses are often more successful than state-owned ones.

Do you think private businesses or nationalized businesses are better for workers?

Which type of business is better for customers?

Controlling Industry

Socialist governments control private ownership by taking industries into public ownership, or nationalizing them. Nationalized industries are managed in the interest of the workers and the state. They are owned and run by the government. When they make profits, this money goes to the government to help fund public services that benefit the whole country. The workers benefit too because they are paid a good salary, are entitled to paid vacation, and also receive sick pay.

The Government Pays

However, when things go badly for nationalized industries, the cost of this must then be covered by the government. Where private businesses might reduce their costs by employing fewer people, businesses in public ownership are under pressure to look after their workers. Critics of socialism argue that this makes them very inefficient. They argue that a business run mainly to benefit its workers will not be able to respond to changing conditions.

PEOPLE AND POLITICS

Charles Dickens (1812–1870) was an English novelist and social critic living in the nineteenth century. In his 15 novels, and other works, he exposed social injustice and inequality in Victorian Britain. His stories are full of examples of poverty, exploitation, and oppression at the hands of the wealthy. Dickens tried to highlight the need for empathy and compassion when working toward a more just and equal society. The novelist advocated for social reform to improve people's quality of life. He believed that the wealthy and the government had a moral responsibility to take action to help the poor.

Charles Dickens

Damaging Ordinary Lives

Socialists argue that without government control, most ordinary people's opportunities in life will be damaged by the actions of a few wealthy or powerful people. For this reason, socialist governments are involved in many areas of people's lives, from education to healthcare.

Targets for Money

In places where most businesses are owned and run by the country's government, each industry may have targets for how much money it makes, and how workers are paid and treated. In nonsocialist countries, there may also be general targets, or rules, about how workers should be paid that cover all industries. For example, many countries have a minimum wage that all workers should be paid, but this is likely to be higher under a socialist government.

Damaging the Country

Critics of socialism argue that socialist "big government" makes a country less successful. By telling people how they must live their lives, socialists stop them from acting on their own individual initiative. If people are allowed to act on their own, they come up with new ideas that create wealth and jobs. Huge governments are not good at coming up with these types of new ideas and, therefore, individuals may be held back under a socialist government.

PEOPLE AND POLITICS

Henry Ford (1863–1947) was a businessman who founded the Ford Motor Company in 1903. He is credited with making cars more affordable for ordinary Americans, with the use of a new factory process. Instead of making cars individually, workers repeated tasks in an "assembly line," dramatically reducing the time taken to manufacture cars and therefore their overall cost.

Henry Ford

This image shows workers on a Ford assembly line in 1913.

Socialism in Action

These are the words of Henry Ford:

> "The commonest laborer who sweeps the floor shall receive his $5 per day. We believe in making 20,000 men prosperous and contented rather than ... making a few slave drivers in our establishment millionaires."

Henry Ford is not usually known as a socialist but he decided to pay his workers twice as much as other carmakers, and it worked. His workers were happy to work and, therefore, worked harder and faster, resulting in the production of more cars. The price of the cars dropped, which meant that the workers could also afford to buy the vehicles themselves.

Why do you think Henry Ford decided to pay his workers more money?

PAST AND PRESENT:

Can you see examples of entrepreneurs today who take a similar approach to Henry Ford—paying their workers more to ensure better productivity and wider prosperity?

Education for All?

We take for granted that all young people in western countries will have the opportunity to go to school until their late teenage years, without having to pay for it. However, this was not always the case. And in many poorer parts of the world, free education is still not available.

Educate for Equality

Elementary schooling for all children was introduced around the time socialist ideas were being developed. Since then, levels of education have continued to rise, even in countries such as the United States, where socialists have not held power. Socialists see public education as a way to increase equality in society. If people are educated equally, they are equally able to get good jobs or start businesses. That ensures a more equal standard of living.

Socialism in Action

When socialist governments promise to spend more on health, education, and welfare, whose money are they spending? They are spending money collected from the people through taxes. In a socialist system, taxes are likely to be much higher for wealthy people than they are for poorer people. In effect, richer people pay more for services.

Do you think it is fair that the higher-earning people in society pay more for public services than those people who earn less? Give reasons for your answer.

In many parts of the world, accessing good education is still difficult. These children go to a makeshift school in New Delhi, India.

Health for All

The communist government of the Soviet Union introduced free healthcare for all citizens soon after the Russian Revolution. This was followed by other public healthcare systems, particularly in the years after World War II, when the British NHS was created. Other countries, such as the United States and Canada, provide free healthcare to certain groups, such as the elderly. In developed countries where there is no free healthcare for younger citizens, most people must buy medical insurance to ensure they have access to healthcare.

Care in Cuba

Prior to 1960, Cuba had a poor record on healthcare and education. Giving people full access to these services has led to great improvements, despite the country's many other problems. However, the vast cost of providing free public services for everyone is causing many countries to cut back on the services they provide. Healthcare may be "free" but people often have to resort to a paid option to get the treatment or operations that they need.

PEOPLE AND POLITICS

In the aftermath of World War II, Prime Minister Clement Attlee (1883–1967) oversaw the establishment of a social welfare programme in Britain, including the creation of a free NHS. Britain was the first western country to offer free medical care for every citizen. The country faced grave problems at the time including debt, a housing crisis, and food shortages. The working population paid more in taxes to help pay for this new service.

Giving Workers Power

The early socialists wanted to replace capitalism with a more equal society, in which power would be handed over to the workers. While communist regimes in many countries achieved this goal, many socialists were appalled by the lack of freedom under these regimes. They did not want to create similar systems in their own countries. Instead, social democrats tried to change capitalism to meet the needs of their workers, rather than replacing this political system entirely. One of the key ways they did so was through organizations called trade unions.

The Role of Trade Unions

Trade unions had an important role in limiting the power of capitalism and were often directly linked to socialist political parties. Individually, workers have little power as they can lose their jobs if they complain about pay and conditions. However, if workers come together and unite they have more power because there are more of them. For example, if workers are not happy about an issue, such as pay or conditions, they can stop work and strike to get what they want. Trade unions have had a big influence in shaping the rights that workers in many industries now enjoy, such as paid vacations and a limit to the number of hours that employees must work each week.

This image captures a protest in Germany. It shows workers demanding higher pay.

The Women's Land Army in the United States and the UK was established during World War I and World War II. During that time, women began to contribute greatly to the economy as workers.

Socialism in Action

In recent decades, the power of trade unions has lessened in many areas. There are several reasons why this change has taken place:

- Industries in many developed countries have changed.
- Fewer people are working in big factories and heavy industries.
- Many businesses are more global, so work can be moved overseas.
- Politicians have passed new laws to limit the power of unions.

Can you think of other reasons why unions are less powerful?

PAST AND PRESENT:

Do you think there will be a place for trade unions in the future or do you think they will fade away? Give reasons for your answer.

Rights for Women

In the past, trade unions were often hostile to women workers, who might take men's jobs or work for lower wages. Traditionally, women were expected to run a home and to raise children. But during World War I and World War II, women were required to step-up to help the war effort at home, working in factories and on farms. They proved their capability and attitudes toward women began to change. In recent decades, many more women have worked outside the home. Many feminist groups have used socialist arguments in their attempts to win equal working rights.

CHAPTER 4

Life Under Socialism

Socialism has had an impact on many countries, even those without a socialist government or popular socialist party. Socialist measures, such as free healthcare, can help to safeguard members of society who simply cannot afford health insurance. But what is it like to live in a country that is run by a socialist government?

Ending Poverty and Corruption

Hugo Chavez promised an end to poverty and corruption when he was elected as president of Venezuela in 1998. When he died in 2013, he was mourned by millions of Venezuelans, although he had as many enemies as friends. Chavez was elected, but made sure that he filled important jobs within his government with his friends, to ensure loyalty. He also quickly broke the rules when he needed to hold on to power.

Socialism for the Twenty-First Century

In 2006, Chavez introduced what he called "twenty-first century socialism" in Venezuela. The socialist leader had previously announced "missions" to make healthcare and adult education available to the poor in Venezuela. His successes included reducing the country's level of unemployment, cutting the number of people living in extreme poverty, and improving healthcare so fewer Venezuelans died in infancy and childhood.

Reliance on Oil

But Chavez's successes relied on Venezuela's oil wealth. Exports of oil more than quadrupled between 1999 and 2011. On Chavez's death, Vice President Nicolas Maduro came to power. He continued Chavez's policies, but when oil prices dropped in 2015, Venezuela's economy tumbled. The government had to make cuts to public spending and poverty rose significantly. Corruption within the country has also continued with Maduro largely working with relatives and close friends.

Hugo Chavez

Socialism in Action

South America is one part of the world where socialist parties have had a degree of success. Venezuela formed alliances with socialist governments in Bolivia and Ecuador. Brazil, the largest country in the region, has also elected socialist governments. South American countries have often faced big social inequalities. Many countries have a few very rich people but extreme poverty for much of the population.

Why do you think people have elected socialist governments in South America?

What impact do you think a country's wealth has on the choice a government makes?

PAST AND PRESENT:

In many countries around the world, the divide between the wealthy and the poor in society has grown in recent years. Do you think it is likely that this will spark a new wave of socialism? Give reasons for your answer.

A shanty town in Caracas, the capital of Venezuela, where extreme poverty is still prevalent.

A Perfect System?

Hugo Chavez's regime in Venezuela was an example of a socialist system that achieved good, but was flawed in many ways. There are similar examples in recent history. Many extreme socialist or communist governments have been a disaster for the people they claimed to help. In the 1970s and 1980s, the Vietnamese faced famine after their communist government made the transportation of food and goods between provinces illegal, and took control of businesses and farms. Many people were forced to work on the land and thousands were executed when they tried to escape.

Revolution and War

Extreme socialist regimes usually arise from revolution and war, such as the government of the Soviet Union after 1917 and Fidel Castro's Cuba after 1959. While they may have achieved success in some areas, such as improving education, there have been major drawbacks. Central planning and nationalization of industries may have created more equality, but people have often faced poverty. Communist states, from East Germany to North Korea, have also restricted the freedom and human rights of their people. Opponents of socialism often cite these human rights issues when criticizing the political system.

Socialism in Action

Even democratic socialism faces criticism. Supporters of pure capitalism argue that humans are naturally competitive and selfish. We will always try to beat the system or gain power. The idea that all people will cooperate in a socialist society is doomed to fail.

Some people argue that countries that practice socialism may provide benefits and security for their people, but this normally involves the loss of some personal freedom (even if it is just the freedom to get rich). What do you think?

Capitalists also argue that giving extra rights to workers will eventually lead to job losses, because of competition from other countries. Do you agree with this argument?

PAST AND PRESENT:

As well as questioning whether socialism can ever be successful, we should also ask the same questions about capitalism. Can a system that allows huge inequality between rich and poor really be the best option? Do you think either capitalism or socialism have a place in modern society? Give reasons for your answer.

PEOPLE AND POLITICS

Extreme socialism in North Korea has been led by one family for over 75 years. The nation was founded in 1948 in the aftermath of World War II, and Kim Il-sung (1912–1994) became its "great leader." He was succeeded by his son, Kim Jong-il (1941–2011) and his grandson Kim Jong-un. These leaders have strived for economic self-sufficiency and military independence for their isolated nation, but the country has constant struggles with poverty and food shortages.

In North Korea, Kim Il-sung and Kim Jong-il are still revered as the nation's "great leaders."

Growing Fear of Socialism

In the decades after World War II, the United States, and other capitalist countries, were very concerned that the Soviet Union wanted to spread communism and socialism across the world. The United States, and its allies, opposed the Soviet Union in a drawn-out political struggle that became known as the Cold War.

Lech Wałęsa was awarded the Nobel Peace Prize in 1983.

Total Control

During this time, many countries in the West also elected socialist governments. Socialist governments that sprang up after World War II were often oppressive. The socialist governments in Eastern Europe did everything they could to prevent protests by their own people, including the use of secret police and military force. In 1980, Polish workers formed an independent trade union, called Solidarity, and went on strike at a shipyard in the city of Gdansk. They wanted better working conditions and more political freedom. Strikes broke out across Poland and sowed the seeds for the end of communism in the country. Solidarity leader, Lech Wałęsa, became the first freely elected president of Poland in 1990.

Capitalists against Socialism

Those who oppose socialism strongly are often the people who benefit most from capitalism, such as business leaders. However, many poorer people also believe that government should not interfere in people's lives. Less interference means lower taxes—and that means more money for individuals to spend.

Socialism in Action

In an interview, author John Steinbeck (1902–1968) once suggested that socialism did not become embedded in the United States because poor Americans see themselves not as an oppressed class but as temporarily embarrassed millionaires! Steinbeck was trying to answer the question why socialism has never become a big political force in the United States. His suggestion was that Americans believed they could all become rich and did not accept the idea of a struggle between the working class and capitalism.

Although the United States has never been run under a socialist government, can you think of areas of socialism that the country has embraced?

PAST AND PRESENT: Can you imagine a scenario in which the United States could adopt more socialist policies? What might that be?

PEOPLE AND POLITICS

John Steinbeck was a novelist whose stories of 1930s United States depicted the lives of the working class and migrant workers, and their exploitation at the hands of the wealthy. His calls for social justice were met with controversy and criticism by some, but he won the Nobel Prize for literature in 1962 for his "realistic writing" and "social perception."

John Steinbeck

CHAPTER 5

The Future of Socialism

Socialism faced its greatest crisis in the 1990s, after the collapse of communist governments in Eastern Europe and the Soviet Union. Some governments still claimed to be socialist or communist, such as in China. However, most economies started to move toward a capitalist system. Is socialism now an idea that has had its day, or does the system still have a future?

Adapting to Change

In developed countries, such as those in western Europe, socialist parties have learned to adapt. Many leading politicians have argued that equality and welfare are just as important to people as they always had been, but socialist ideas about workers controlling factories cannot deliver a sustainable system of government. In the 1990s, politicians proposed a "third way" of governing fairly—a middle ground between socialism and capitalism. Leaders who argued for this "third way" included President Bill Clinton and British prime minister Tony Blair. Although it was a successful strategy at the time, it was dependent on a period of economic growth that helped to fund increased social spending. When the economy turned, inequality rose again.

PEOPLE AND POLITICS

Joe Biden was a supporter of the "third way" in the 1990s, but by the time of his presidency in 2021, world circumstances had changed. The global financial crisis of 2008, rising inequality, and the COVID-19 pandemic, called for a different approach. During his time in office, Biden raised social spending, lowered the cost of healthcare, invested in infrastructure, and increased taxes on the wealthy to help redistribute wealth. Some people believe these policies were a move further toward socialism, but others say Biden simply revived democratic capitalism by investing in an economy that brings greater opportunities to American workers.

Beyond the West

Beyond the western world, the story has been different. In developing countries, where many people live in poverty, heavy industry has increased. Many people are now employed in industry, but still live in poverty with very few workplace rights. In countries such as Venezuela, where workers often have few rights, socialist governments have taken power. It is likely that countries such as these will remain socialist for the foreseeable future.

This man works in Venezuela's oil industry. In recent years, trade unionists have been arrested in the country for trying to achieve fairer employment conditions.

Socialism in Action

The way people work has changed. The mines and factories in Europe and North America, where socialist ideas took hold, have closed or moved overseas. People are now more likely to work in call centers or huge grocery stores. Most workers in developed countries are no longer part of a trade union.

How do you think job changes have affected socialist ideas?

Do you think people are still interested in issues such as equality and having a say in their workplace?

People took to the streets of Athens, Greece, in 2010 to protest against austerity measures in the wake of the 2008 financial crisis.

Unfair Banking

As communist regimes collapsed in many parts of the world in the 1990s, it seemed as if capitalism had beaten socialism. However, in the years after 2008, capitalism faced a crisis that caused some people to question the system itself. The crisis started when people discovered that banks had taken huge risks in lending money to people who could not repay it. This included lending to people to buy houses that they couldn't afford. The banking system is so complex that many of these risks had been passed on to other banks all over the world—without the banks being aware of this.

Disaster in the System

Governments in the United States, Europe, and elsewhere had to give the banks billions of dollars to make up for their catastrophic losses. People were angry when they saw the enormous sums of money they had paid in taxes being given to high-earning bankers. Some banks were even nationalized in some countries in a bid to resolve the problem.

Economic Crisis

The banking crisis caused such huge problems in the world economy that many people lost their jobs and their homes. People expressed their anger in mass demonstrations that criticized the capitalist system. While some claimed the 2008 recession proved the flaws in capitalism, many governments reacted by cutting spending on social welfare, and other services, in an attempt to reduce their countries' enormous debts.

Global Concerns

During the 2020s, various events have rocked the global economy. They include the COVID-19 pandemic, US-China trade tensions, and war in Ukraine and Gaza. Many people believe these difficulties could encourage societies to become more polarized in their political views over the coming years.

Socialism in Action

The richest 10 percent of Americans own more than two-thirds of all the country's wealth. And during the COVID-19 pandemic, the wealth of the top 1 percent increased by more than a third, primarily due to the success of stocks and private businesses. Because the wealthy can afford to save and invest more of their money, it causes stock prices to rise, and that further increases wealth inequality.

Some say inequality is inevitable, because people are not equally intelligent and hardworking. Do you agree or disagree? Give reasons for your answer.

What do you think could be done to reduce inequality?

The COVID-19 pandemic and imposed lockdowns around the world saw a sharp downturn in global finances.

CONCLUSION

Socialism Past, Present, and Future

We have learned that socialism comes in many forms, but all socialists share some common beliefs. We know that socialist ideas have existed since ancient times. However, the detailed theories that are the basis of socialism developed fully during the Industrial Revolution, particularly in the writings of Karl Marx and Friedrich Engels.

Complex Ideas

We have discovered the different ways that revolutionary socialists and social democrats seek to gain power, and the key differences between socialism and capitalism. We know about socialist ideas such as public ownership of industries and central planning, and both the benefits and drawbacks of these ideas. We have also discovered how people have opposed socialist ideas.

When livelihoods are at risk, political protests become more prevalent as people's opinions become divided.

As times change, our shared humanity may guide the political principles we adopt.

Socialism in Action

Aleksandr Solzhenitsyn (1918–2008), a Russian activist, once said:

> "Human beings are born with different capacities. If they are free, they are not equal. And if they are equal, they are not free."

What do you think Solzhenitsyn meant by these words?

Why might socialism be a suitable form of government in some parts of the world and not in others?

PAST AND PRESENT:

What do you think drives some governments today to take aspects of both socialism and capitalism to solve their country's problems?

Changing Times

We have also seen how changing circumstances over the decades have affected political views in different parts of the world. In times of economic certainty, socialism has worked well, as Venezuela found in the 2000s when its oil wealth aided social spending. We have seen that extreme forms of socialism emerged in countries facing revolution and uncertainty, such as in Russia and North Korea. And we have seen how different governments have adopted aspects of socialism in their policies. Some people see socialism as a way of reducing wealth inequality, while others feel socialism restricts the freedom of individuals and countries to develop and prosper.

Socialism in the Future?

The years since the early 1990s have been difficult ones for socialism around the world, as governments have changed and adapted. The global impact of the 2008 financial crisis as well as the COVID-19 pandemic, trade tensions, and international conflict, have led governments to reassess domestic policies in the best interests of their citizens. Rising inequality may lead to renewed interest in socialism as a way of organizing society.

Glossary

ally a country that supports another one

bureaucrat a government official

capital money that is invested in something

capitalism an economic system in which a country's trade and industry are controlled by private owners for profit

citizen a member of a country

Cold War the state of hostility that existed between the United States and Soviet Union, and their allies, between 1945 and 1990

communist a person or political party that believes all property should be controlled by the government, with everyone working for the state

corruption making illegal payments to public officials, or others, in exchange for receiving special treatment

democracy a system in which the government is voted for by most, or all, of the adults in that country

developed country a country in which industry and the economy are still developing. The average wealth of people in developing countries is usually less than that of people in developed countries

dictatorship rule by an unelected person, or group, who have seized power, for example, after a revolution

entrepreneur a person who starts a business in order to make a profit

equality having the same rights and opportunities as other people

fascist a strongly nationalist or extreme right-wing political party or government

feminist a person who believes in equal rights for women

human rights rights that every human being has, regardless of their race, sex, or religion

independence standing on its own. When a country is independent it has its own government

Industrial Revolution a period of huge change that began in Britain in the 1700s. During this period, enormous development in industry and manufacturing took place

industrialist a person who owns a factory or large industrial business

manufactured anything that is made by people from raw materials, such as goods made in a factory

political party a group of people with similar ideas about how a country should be run

propaganda the spreading of information to influence public opinion or present the person creating the information in a favorable way

public ownership when industries or businesses are owned by the government and operated for the benefit of all people in a country

revolution a violent upheaval to overthrow a ruler or bring about radical change

sanctions trade or other restrictions imposed on a country by the international community in order to force its government to change their policy

secret police security officers who maintain security within a country

Soviet Union a union of countries in eastern Europe, led by Russia, which lasted until 1991

trade unions organizations made up of all workers in a business or industry, to give them more bargaining power with employers than they would have individually

Find Out More

Books

Adams, Sabrina. *Equality, Social Justice, and our Future* (Spotlight on our Future). Rosen Publishing Group, 2022.

Morlock, Rachael. *Equality and Social Justice* (Spotlight on Global Issues). Rosen Publishing Group, 2022.

Uhl, Xina M. *Communism* (Examining Political Systems). Rosen Publishing Group, 2020.

Websites

Learn more about socialism at:
education.nationalgeographic.org/resource/socialism

Take a look at communism and socialism and the differences between them at:
www.coolkidfacts.com/communism-vs-socialism

Find out more about how socialism works at:
https://money.howstuffworks.com/socialism.htm

Publisher's note to educators and parents:
All the websites featured above have been carefully reviewed to ensure that they are suitable for students. However, many websites change often, and we cannot guarantee that a site's future contents will continue to meet our high standards of educational value. Please be advised that students should be closely monitored whenever they access the Internet.

Index

About the Author

Alex Webb has written many children's books and has a particular interest in history and politics. She has found researching and writing this book fascinating and hopes that it helps students everywhere gain knowledge and insight into political systems and how they work.